LightBox

EXPRESSIONS OF HOPE *from* YOUNG WOMEN *in the* KIBERA SLUM OF NAIROBI

Photographs and Essays by the Members of the Binti Pamoja Center in Nairobi, Kenya

EDITED BY **EMILY VERELLEN** • FORWARD BY **CAROL BELLAMY**

The Binti Pamoja Center
a program of Carolina for Kibera
www.bintipamoja.org

LightBox: Expressions of Hope From Young Women in the Kibera Slum of Nairobi
Photographs and Essays by the Members of the Binti Pamoja Center in Nairobi, Kenya
Forward by Carol Bellamy
Edited, produced and published by Emily Verellen in New York, NY

Cover and book design by Allyson Murphy. For more information
on her graphic design work, please visit *www.allysonmurphy.com*

The Binti Pamoja Center is a program of Carolina for Kibera (CFK).
CFK is a U.S. non-profit 501(c)(3) charitable corporation.
For more information on CFK, please visit *http://cfk.unc.edu*

Binti Pamoja Center Co-Founders: Emily Verellen and Karen Austrian
Binti Pamoja Center Program Coordinator: Caroline Sakwa
Carolina for Kibera Program Manager: Salim Mohamed
Carolina for Kibera Founder: Rye Barcott

LightBox has been funded in full through a grant from The Fledgling Fund. Through its
Creative Media Initiative, The Fledgling Fund supports film, photography, web-based and printed
media projects that have the power to stimulate social change. The Fledgling Fund is pleased to support
LightBox, which not only bears witness to the issues faced by the young women of Binti Pamoja,
but also demonstrates their resilience and hope.
For more information about The Fledgling Fund, please visit *www.thefledglingfund.org*

100% of the proceeds from *LightBox* support the Binti Pamoja Center Scholarship Fund,
which helps Binti Pamoja members attend high school. For more information, to order additional copies
or to make a tax-deductible donation, please visit *www.bintipamoja.org* or *http://cfk.unc.edu*

ISBN 0-9778741-0-9

LightBox was printed in Hong Kong by Regal Printing

Cover image: Photograph by Celestine, Binti Pamoja Center member, age 19.

LightBox *is dedicated to every member of The Binti Pamoja Center – past, present and future.*

Your tenacious strength, beautiful spirit and relentless energy are a constant inspiration.

Never stop believing in yourselves.

And for my mom, Cristy. Your passion for life is radiant.

Binti Pamoja Center Members

Photo by Emily Verellen

LightBox

A light box is a tool photographers use to examine a negative.
The brilliance of a negative depends on the light in which the photograph was taken and in which it is viewed.
Without that light, the image is distorted and incomplete.
A light box illuminates the positive parts of a negative and creates a more vivid image.

Mainstream news about Kenya, and most developing nations, is overwhelmingly negative.
These photographs, and the accompanying essays, are a light through which we see the complete picture.
These young Kenyan women used disposable or simple point-and-shoot cameras to create and share candid messages about their magnificent hope and perseverance, despite the tremendous obstacles in their lives.
The truth is that the positive far outweighs and outlasts the negative.
We need to adjust our ability to seek out and absorb the light. Their light.
This is their book, and these are their photographs.

Acknowledgments

I offer my most sincere gratitude to the following people for their heartfelt support of this project. Your ideas, guidance and resources were the most wonderful gifts.

To the Binti Pamoja members who made this book possible, infinite thanks for offering your beautiful voices and ideas to the Binti Pamoja Center, and to this project. You will reach, teach and inspire.

To the families of Binti Pamoja members, thank you for believing in your daughters and for allowing us to know and love them.

To the Kibera community, thank you for offering your stories and for recognizing the value in supporting the ambitions of Binti Pamoja members.

To The Fledgling Fund, I am so grateful for your belief in the young women of Binti Pamoja and this project. Your support for *LightBox* has planted the seed for the future success of Binti Pamoja's members. We are proud to have The Fledgling Fund as a partner.

To Allyson Murphy, *LightBox's* enormously talented and dedicated graphic designer, thank you. Your unwavering commitment, creativity and enthusiasm for this project was unexpected and extraordinary. It was truly my pleasure to share this vision with you and I feel so fortunate to have worked together.

To Carol Bellamy, thank you for offering your words to *LightBox*.

To Karen Austrian, Binti Pamoja Co-Founder, thank you for your friendship, leadership and partnership.

To Caroline Sakwa, Binti Pamoja's Coordinator, you continue to amaze us with your commitment to Binti Pamoja, compassion and thoughtful ideas. It has been an honor to work with you on making those ideas a reality.

To Salim Mohamed, CFK's Program Manager, your wisdom and guidance has been a blessing. Thank you for jumping behind this project.

To Rye Barcott, Kim Chapman, Ben Mshila, and all of the CFK family, thank you for understanding the value of *LightBox* from the beginning and seeing the potential in The Binti Pamoja Center.

To the late Tabitha Festo, CFK's beloved mother, thank you for your guidance. Your strength is reflected in this book.

To Mary Ann Burris, one of the first voices of encouragement behind *LightBox*, thank you for knowing the power of this project before it was ever born.

To the most supportive people I know, my parents, Tim and Cristy Verellen, thank you for trusting my instincts and letting me find my way. I feel so blessed.

To Betsy Uhrman and Leena Soman, I feel so fortunate to call you my friends. Thank you for helping me to edit this book and for being so supportive. And to all of the CCD, I value each of you and our friendships tremendously. Thank you for your individuality, wisdom and loving guidance.

To Stephie Frommer, your support for me and this project has been astonishing. Thank you for being my editor, event planner, cheerleader and trusted friend all rolled into one.

To Dave Gaglione, thank you for your creative expertise and friendship.

To my Inwood House colleagues, Kathleen, Kathryn and Jamila, thank you for your enthusiastic encouragement from the beginning.

To Darnell Strom, your patient and thoughtful presence throughout this production has been a treasured blessing. Thank you for always being interested in what I care so much about, and for being a constant source of encouragement.

To Andy Block, Ken Biberaj, Samara Barend and Gabe Stulman, thank you for endless laughs and for keeping me balanced in the midst of a huge undertaking.

To Dawn Wohlfarth, thank you for your peaceful and loving friendship.

To Susan Linee, Jessica Lee, Dave Mozersky and Nathan Nelson, thank you for your ideas.

To Binti Pamoja's funders, including The Ford Foundation, The American Jewish World Service, RAINBO Small Grants Project, Reuters Foundation, Population Council, LBC Foundation, Woodward Charitable Foundation, Summit Charitable Foundation, General Motors East Africa, and all of our generous private donors, thank you for giving The Binti Pamoja Center a chance to serve the young women of Kibera.

Contents

Selected Biographies of Binti Pamoja Members

Questions + Answers

FORWARD

BY **CAROL BELLAMY**

Throughout my career in the private and public sectors (including the Peace Corps, UNICEF and now World Learning), I have tried to challenge my colleagues to see the promise of, and the importance of, investing in youth. The natural energy in youth can be a vehicle to their success, if they are given the support they need. Too often, adults fail to listen to the voices of youth – especially girls and young women. In their voices, however, one can find answers, ideas, motivation and truth.

LightBox is an important resource for people who work in the field of international development, particularly those focused on the lives of young women in poverty. So few people ever have the opportunity to speak with these young women. *LightBox* is also a chance to support their dreams through the Binti Pamoja Scholarship Fund.

The Binti Pamoja Center is an example of a successful, community-led resource for young women. These young women are filled with hope. Their voices are powerful, their photography is beautiful and their potential is undeniable. The mission of this book, to help Binti Pamoja members attend school, is a wonderful way to help them fulfill that potential.

This page: Photo by Miriam, 19

KENYA AT A GLANCE

BASIC FACTS

1963 Date of independence

English Official language

Swahili National language

40+ Number of indigenous tribes in Kenya, each with a distinct language and culture.

Religon

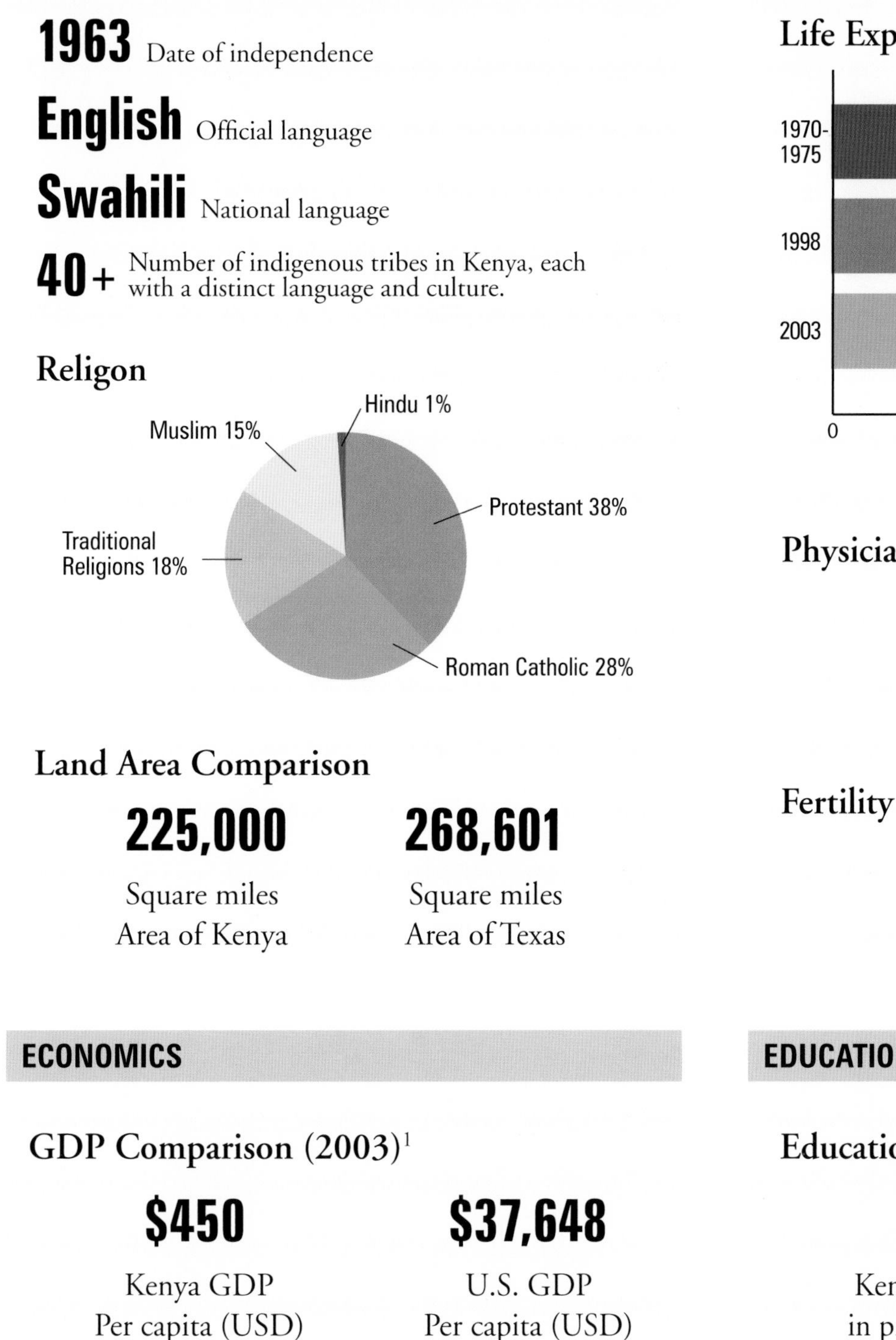

Land Area Comparison

225,000	**268,601**
Square miles Area of Kenya	Square miles Area of Texas

HEALTH

Life Expectancy in Kenya is Declining[1]

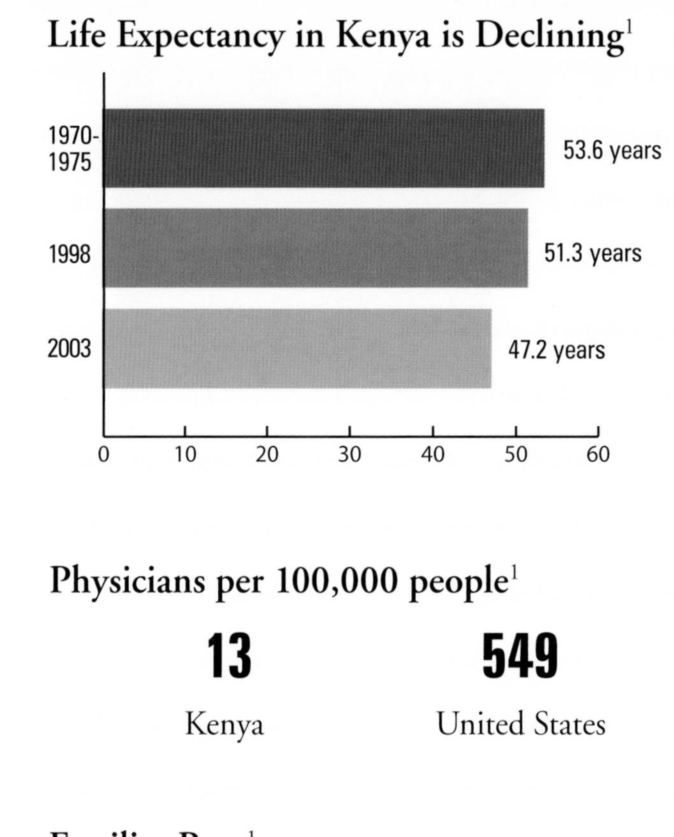

Physicians per 100,000 people[1]

13	**549**
Kenya	United States

Fertility Rate[1]

5.0	**2.0**
Kenya	United States

ECONOMICS

GDP Comparison (2003)[1]

$450	**$37,648**
Kenya GDP Per capita (USD)	U.S. GDP Per capita (USD)

EDUCATION

Education enrollment in Kenya[1]

67%	**25%**
Kenyan children in primary school	Kenyan children in secondary school

[1]UNICEF. *The State of the World's Children.* New York: 2005.

Introduction

BY **EMILY VERELLEN**

Since my first trip to Kenya in 2000, I have found hope, spirit and courage in the voices of the country's women. Their smiles are effervescent. Their beauty is absolute. Their individuality is undeniable. The joy that the women of Kenya have shared with me has been constant, and my sincere wish is that each page of this book will offer you a piece of that joy. As you read their words and see their photographs, I hope you are able to understand their strength and resilience in the face of seemingly insurmountable obstacles. This book demonstrates the inherent potential that lives in the women and youth of Kenya, and reminds us that their energy can lead us to a more equitable, sustainable and peaceful world.

Kibera – The Forgotten City

Kibera is East Africa's largest slum. Located on the outskirts of Nairobi, Kenya's capital, Kibera is approximately the size of New York City's Central Park and is home to nearly one million people, more than one quarter of Nairobi's total population. Although Kibera is one of the most densely populated areas in the world, it does not appear on most Kenyan maps.

I have an intense memory of my first visit to Kibera. My stomach dropped when I reached the peak of the hill above the Kibera valley and saw the sprawling community below me with its sea of mud homes and rusted tin rooftops. As I walked through the narrow dirt pathways between the homes, I desperately tried to absorb everything around me, but felt utterly overwhelmed. Around every corner, I saw smiling children, women cleaning and selling food, bold colored clothing hanging in the bright sunshine and mountains of sludge and trash, seemingly taking over living spaces. I heard giggling babies playing with homemade toys, blaring music, and the calls of boys and girls welcoming me to Kibera. At the same time, my breath was shortened by the smell of burning trash and the dizzying scent of human excrement and rotting refuse. I remember wondering how I would ever describe the dichotomy of this experience to others at home. The joy and suffering. Beauty and filth. Purity and disease.

Kenya is breathtakingly beautiful – the people, the land, the history and the cultures. However, that beauty stands in stark defiance to the consuming reality of poverty, disease and suffering. Fifty-eight percent of Kenya's citizens earn less than $2 a day.[1] As a result, Kenya's population of 33 million is rapidly urbanizing in search of employment, and the promise of a "better life" that is perceived to accompany urban areas. In 1975, 13% of Kenya's population lived in urban areas. By 2002, this number had increased to 39%. By 2015, the United Nations Development Programme estimates that 52% of Kenya's population will live in urban areas, such as Nairobi.[1] As these cities stretch to their limits, more people are pushed to settle in growing slums like Kibera. At least half of Nairobi's citizens already live in slums, which are characterized by a lack of basic services, substandard housing or illegal and inadequate structures, overcrowding, unhealthy and hazardous living conditions, insecurity of tenure or property rights, poverty and social exclusion.

Due to an unresponsive government and unstable economy, Kibera is cramped, filthy and often dangerous. Basic services such as water, electricity, education, health care and sanitation are minimal or non-existent. For example, the pit latrines, which are rarely cleaned, are often shared by hundreds of people. Typical homes in Kibera are 9' x 9', with an average of five people living inside. Water-born diseases such as cholera and typhoid thrive due to the poor sanitation and overcrowding.

Domestic violence, rape and physical assaults are a common part of life for women in Kibera. Women are often treated as property and given little or no opportunity to make decisions about their lives or bodies.

HIV/AIDS and the Need for Comprehensive Reproductive Health Education and Services

Estimates of HIV/AIDS prevalence in Kibera range from 10-25%. This high rate reflects lack of access to, and low use of, contraception, early sexual debut, high rates of prostitution and transactional sex, multiple partners, widespread misinformation about the disease and high rates of forced sex. Those not infected with the disease are still deeply impacted due to its toll on families, the economy, youth, education and employment. Children often bare the heaviest weight of the disease – there are more than 50,000 children orphaned by AIDS in Kibera.[2]

Poverty intensifies the AIDS crisis by significantly reducing access to education, health and sexuality information, testing and basic medical care. The disease disproportionately affects women. In addition to an increased physiological susceptibility to HIV infection, violations of women's rights heighten their vulnerability. Women's subordinate role in marriage, unequal access to economic opportunity and health resources and diminished legal rights are some of the factors that fuel the pandemic.

Approximately 1.2 million Kenyans are living with HIV/AIDS. Women in Kenya, ages 15-24, have double the infection rate of men the same age, and that gap is increasing.[3] As of 2003, only 59% of Kenyan women, ages 15-24, knew that condoms could prevent HIV. The nation's condom prevalence rate is only 39%.[1] There is a pressing need for comprehensive and expanded reproductive health education and services in Kenya.

Denied Access

In Kenya, abortion is illegal, except to protect the life of the pregnant woman. As a result, there are an estimated 300,000 illegal abortions each year in Kenya - over 800 each day. Almost all of these abortions are unsafe, resulting in 20,000 hospitalizations each year. Over 2,600 Kenyan women die due to post-abortion complications annually.[4] Twenty to thirty times that number of women suffer permanent damage.[5] Their stories are never heard.

In 2004, the World Health Organization estimated that there were 19 million unsafe abortions around the world, and 67,900 of those resulted in maternal death.[6] In Africa, the mortality risk from an unsafe abortion is one in 150. In the United States, where abortions are performed legally and safely, the risk of maternal death due to abortion is less than one per 100,000 procedures.[4]

International politics continue to put the lives of women in danger. For example, American policy denies U.S. funding to foreign non-governmental organizations that provide safe abortion services, counseling, referral, or information on safe abortion, or advocate for changes in abortion law in their own country. The net result of this rule cripples efforts to prevent unintended pregnancies by cutting funds to programs that provide family planning education, distribute contraception or provide women's health services. Ironically, these are often programs that do not provide abortion services.

The Value of Education

Around the world, 100 million children are denied their right to an education, and 60% of them are girls. In Sub-Saharan Africa alone, 20 million girls do not go to school.[7] In developing countries where there are school fees, parents are often forced to make a choice. They are more likely to send their son to school than their daughter. The long-term damage of keeping a child home from

school is colossal. Without an education, a girl is often forced into early marriage and pregnancy, or child labor.

In Kenya, where school fees have long been the tradition, primary school fees were abolished in 2002. As a result, an additional 1.2 million children enrolled in school that year alone, an increase of more than 20%.[3] However, for many children, and especially for girls, secondary school is still inaccessible. As you will read in the pages of this book, so many Kenyan youth are eager to attend school, and yet are never given the opportunity.

The Binti Pamoja Center

As I walk through Kibera today, I am still overwhelmed by intense emotions. However, beyond the suffering, I have found hope in the voices, energy and wisdom of the young women of The Binti Pamoja Center.

The Binti Pamoja (*Daughters United* in Swahili) Center is a reproductive health and women's rights program for teenage girls in Kibera, and a program of Carolina for Kibera (CFK). CFK serves approximately 10,000 Kibera residents each year through four major programs: a youth soccer association, The Tabitha Medical Clinic, The Taka ni Pato (*Trash is Cash* in Swahili) youth waste management program and The Binti Pamoja Center. All CFK programs, including Binti Pamoja, are managed by Kenyans with support from U.S.-based volunteers.

Karen Austrian and I founded The Binti Pamoja Center and incorporated it into Carolina for Kibera in 2002 after studying in Kenya in college and recognizing the need for such a program in Kibera. While studying in Kenya, I focused my work on the needs of Nairobi street children and Karen worked with a reproductive health clinic providing community outreach. Working with Nairobi street children, I realized that, while there was an abundance of youth programs, there was a gap in programming specifically for girls. The youth programs that did exist tended to attract boys, due to a reliance on sports programming, overwhelmingly male leadership, and a lack of sensitivity to the domestic responsibilities of young women in Kenya. From her work in the clinic, Karen saw that reproductive health education and outreach largely targeted married women, and missed young women's unique set of needs. After returning home, the powerful experiences that we both had in Kenya left us with a desire to return to Nairobi to implement an innovative program specifically targeting young women.

Themed photography and reflective writing assignments were the initial activities that Karen and I used to engage the young women of The Binti Pamoja Center. Photography was an important tool for fostering discussion because, while describing their images, the young women were able to talk about otherwise taboo subjects. Today, Binti Pamoja uses drama, writing, peer-led small group discussions and photography to explore the critical issues that 13-18-year-old young women face in Kibera. Issues include: HIV/AIDS and other sexually transmitted infections, lack of reproductive health care and information, unintended early pregnancy, violence against women, prostitution, female circumcision, sexual abuse, unequal access to education and stifling domestic responsibilities. In addition, the Center hosts monthly speakers and field trips, a community drama group, a participant-driven newsletter, community service projects, family events, an extensive HIV/AIDS peer education program and other interactive activities.

Caroline Sakwa, a young Kenyan woman, assumed leadership of Binti Pamoja in 2004 and is successfully managing the Center, leading new program developments and mentoring the 60 members. The Binti Pamoja Center has created a safe space for teenage girls to harness their energy, sense of hope and mutual understanding to proactively affect change in their community. And it's working. The young women of The Binti Pamoja Center have become proud leaders in their community in the fight against HIV/AIDS, violence against women and unequal access to education, and they have learned how to take control over their reproductive health. They have become the leaders they were seeking.

LightBox

LightBox is comprised entirely of photographs taken by Binti Pamoja's members and essays they have written to accompany those photos. All of the pictures were taken with disposable or simple point-and-shoot cameras during the period of 2002-2004, when Karen and I were managing the program in Kibera. Most of the photographers had never before held a camera, and we provided less than two hours of basic training. The quality of the photographs in this book is not perfect. However, their expressions offer a candid look at the lives of young women in poverty.

The young women in this book are not an accurate representation of all young women in Kibera. These young women exude a unique confidence and mission-driven attitude that is rare in their community, and is in large part due to their participation in Binti Pamoja. *LightBox* demonstrates the value of empowering a young woman and is a celebration of the victories these young women achieve every day. Their photography and essays display a powerful message – one of struggle, perseverance and hope.

LightBox is representative of Binti Pamoja's commitment to the futures of our members. Because the production of *LightBox* was fully funded by a grant from The Fledgling Fund, 100% of the funds raised from *LightBox* support The Binti Pamoja Center Scholarship Fund. This scholarship fund helps active Binti Pamoja members attend high school, which is often out of reach because of school fees. Before receiving the scholarship of approximately USD $150 per year, Binti Pamoja's staff meets with the member's family to ensure that they are committed to sending their daughter to school. Families sign a contract stating their support for their daughter's education and agree to provide the few remaining costs of education not covered by the scholarship fund.

Purchasing *LightBox* is a tangible way to show your support for the ambitions of young women in Kibera. So many of us take our education for granted while girls around the world would give anything to enter a classroom and be told that their future is important. On behalf of Binti Pamoja members and staff, I thank you for giving them that chance.

The graceful voices of Binti Pamoja are my well of inspiration. I draw upon their intelligence, humor, courage and determination every day. It is one of my greatest joys to share this book with you. I believe their words have relevance for men and women around the world, of all ages, and from every walk of life. My hope is that, as a result of *LightBox,* you will keep their voices with you and feel inspired by their lives and what their futures hold.

---

[1] UNDP. *Human Development Report 2005.* New York: United Nations Development Programme, 2005.
[2] UNICEF. *Fighting AIDS on the Football Field.* New York: UNICEF, 2001.
[3] SIECUS. *PEPFAR Country Profiles: Focusing in on Prevention and Youth.* 2005.
[4] Gebreselassie, H., et. al. "The Magnitude of Abortion Complications in Kenya." *BJOG: An International Journal of Obstetrics and Gynecology.* September 2005, Vol. 112 (1229-1235).
[5] Kaisernetwork.org. *Illegal Abortion in Kenya, Where Procedure Is Allowed Only When Pregnancy Endangers Health, Life of Women. Daily Reports.* The Henry J. Kaiser Family Foundation, April 28, 2005.
[6] World Health Organization. *Unsafe Abortion: Fourth Edition.* Geneva: World Health Organization, 2004.
[7] Save the Children. *60 Million Girls.* London: Save the Children, 2005.

Kibera Geography

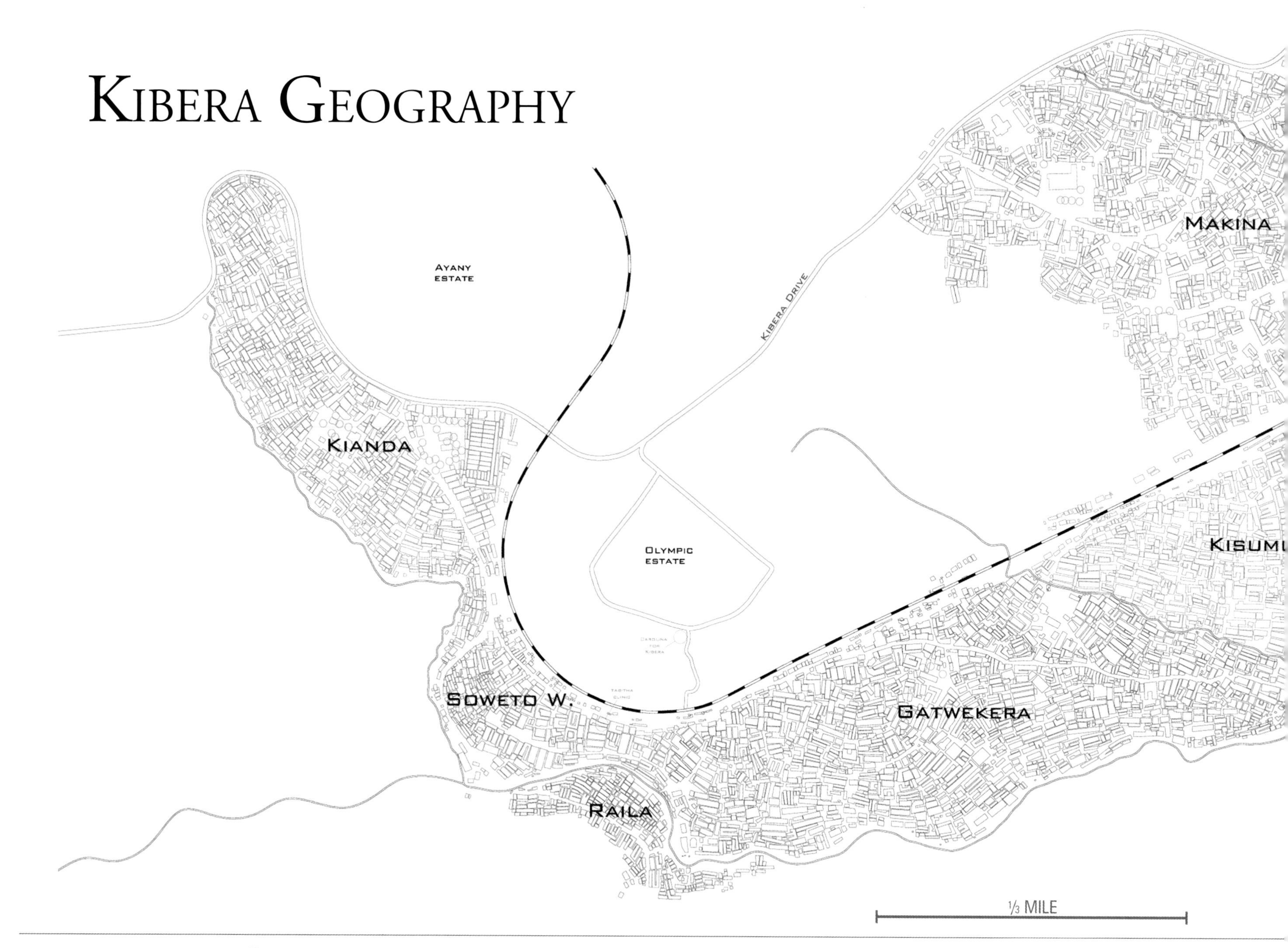

One of the world's largest slums, Kibera is located within walking distance of the highrise buildings of downtown Nairobi. Kibera, a Nubian word for "Forest," was originally settled by Sudanese soldiers after fighting with the British in World War I. After Kenya's independence in 1963, urban areas expanded rapidly, without corresponding infrastructure such as housing, roads and sanitation. Basic services such as water, electricity, education, health care and sanitation are minimal or non-existent. Today, Kibera is home to many of Kenya's 43 tribes and has seen bloody tribal conflict in the recent past.

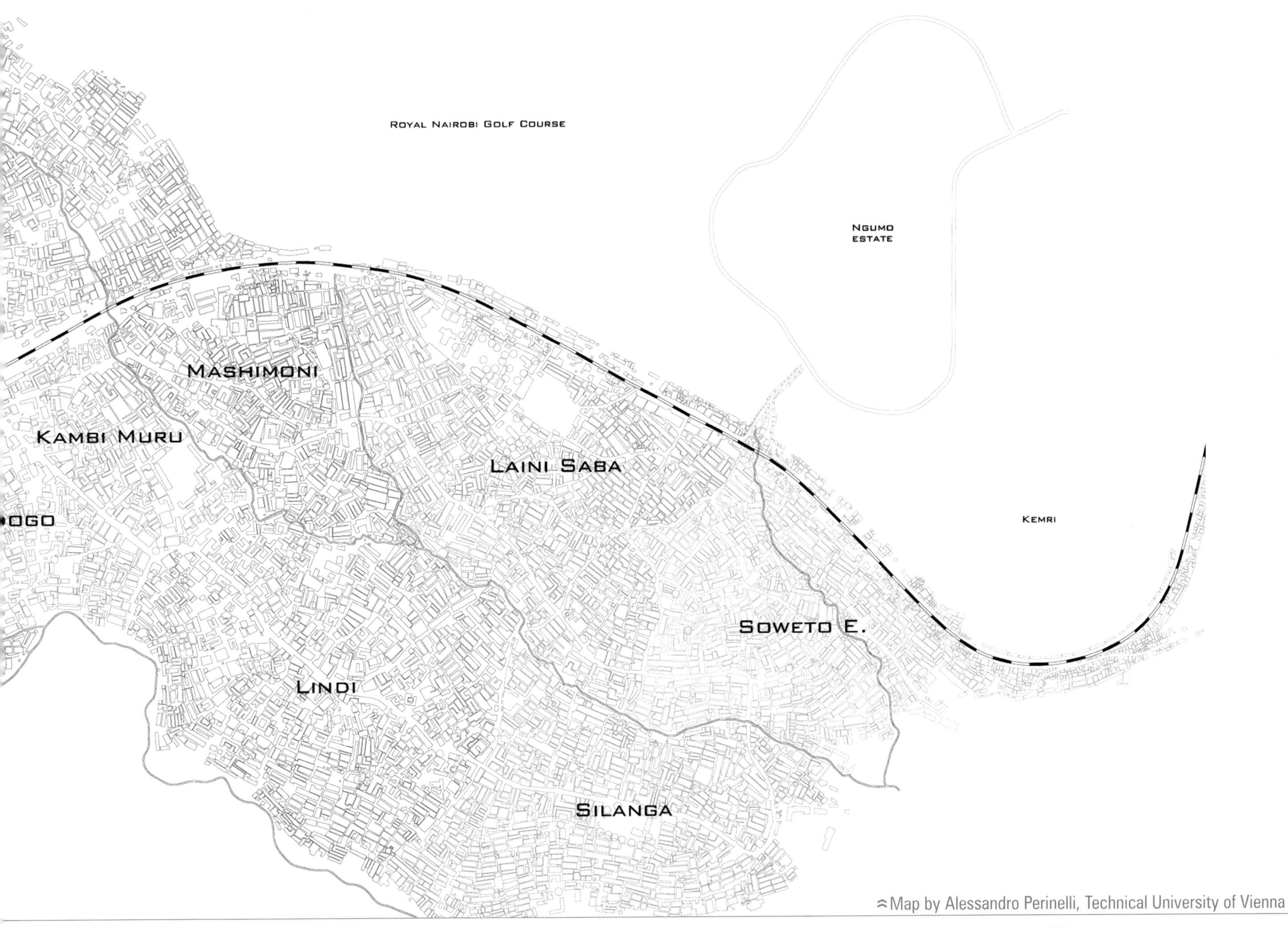

≈Map by Alessandro Perinelli, Technical University of Vienna

Although Kibera is only a few square miles large, it is home to nearly one million people. Kenyans migrate to Nairobi in search of employment and perceived better access to services. However, what they find is that Kibera, and similar slums, are the only places they can afford to live. Kibera is made up of a massive conglomerate of "villages," all connected by a labyrinth of dirt paths. There are no streets or house numbers. Most Kibera homes are approximately 9' by 9' and have at least five people living inside. Water-born diseases such as cholera and typhoid are common. Estimates of HIV/AIDS prevalence in Kibera range from 10-25%.

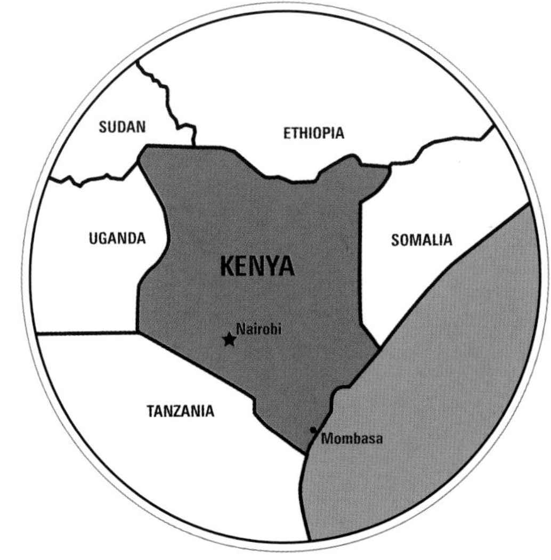

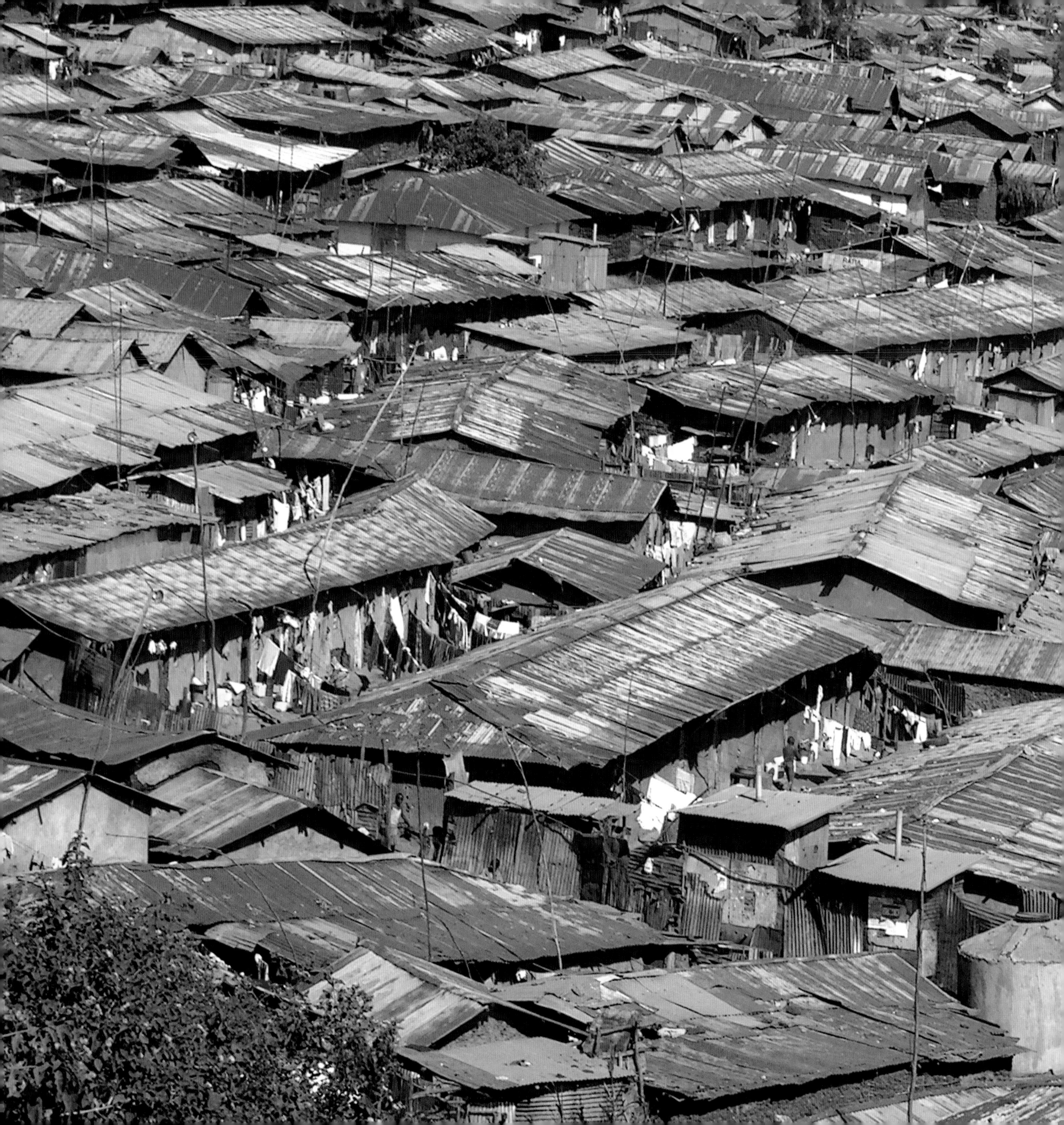

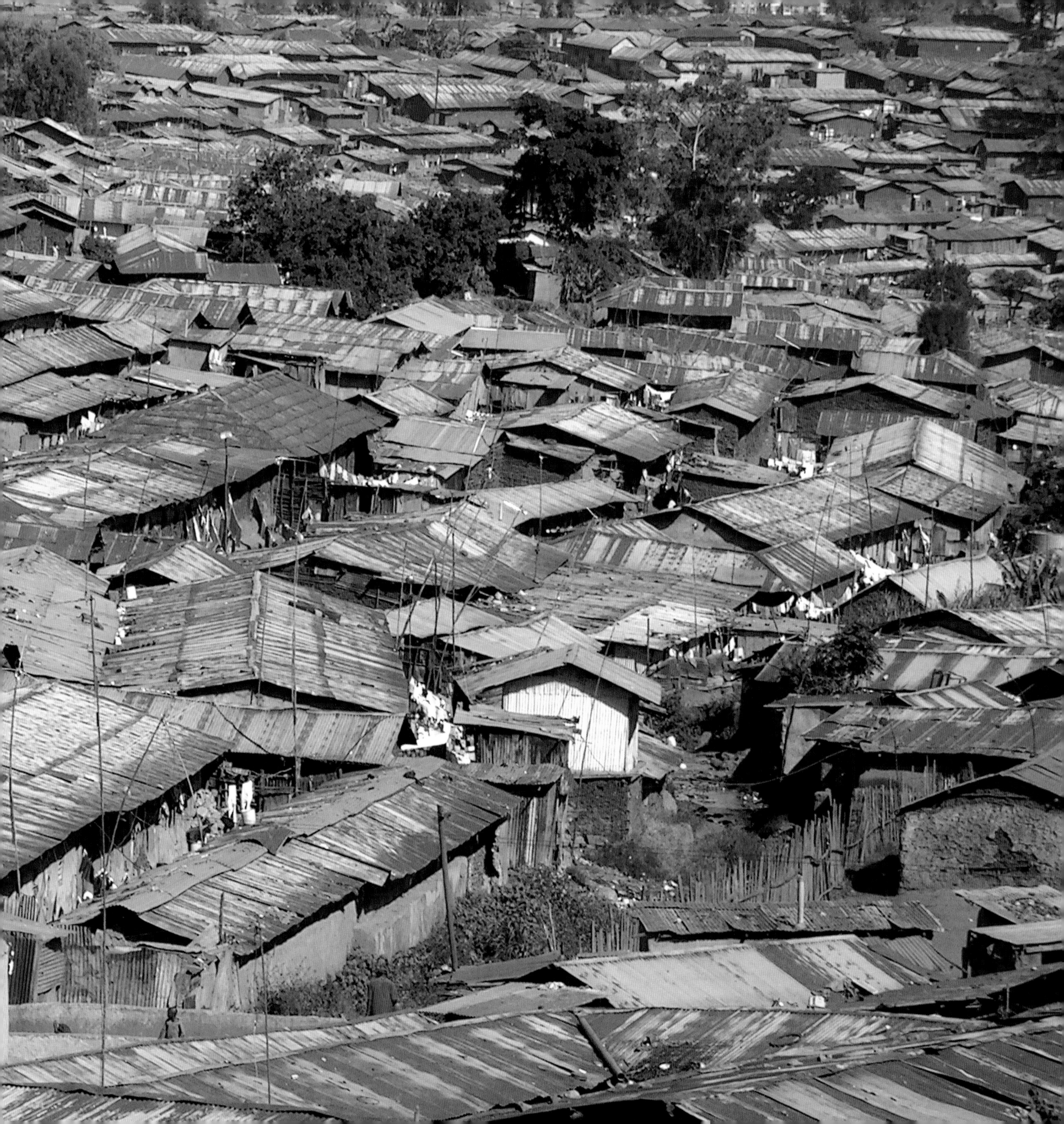

Life in Kibera seems to be hard. You see, this woman is pregnant and she also has a young baby who she should take care of, instead of being pregnant. You know, many women in Kibera don't have their own husbands, so they go in a bar, and get a man with a beer and start talking with them because they know that the man has money. At that time, they will start drinking together. And don't forget, she has a baby at home. So at the last minute, the man will tell her to pay for his beer, and when she tells him that she doesn't have the money, the man will tell her to pay with her body. She will agree to pay with her body so she can be released. So you see, women can become pregnant because of money. So, that is a problem for women in Kibera.

MOURINE A., 18

≈ Previous pages: Photo by Celestine, 19
« Opposite page: Photo by Mourine A., 18

CELESTINE, 19

My name is Celestine. I'm the second born in our family. I like my family very much, especially my mother who has taken me to school from nursery to now in high school. My mother is the one who pays for my school fees, and anything that I need I get from her. I thank God for my beautiful and kind mother who always listens to me.

My mom is a business woman. She tries her best to pay school fees for all of us in school. She does not want us to be sent home from school without fees. Even when I am sent home because of uniform and school fees, I know my mother tried very hard to get for me that money. I love both my parents, but mostly my mother who always keeps me.

« Opposite page: Photo by Celestine, 19

This girl is called Wamboi and she is nine years old. Her mother doesn't have any food and the girl wanted money to pay for school. So her mother left the girl outside here to sell those things so that she can get money to pay for school. This child is young and she is selling onions and eggs. She doesn't even know how to give the change back to customers. A young child like this girl is supposed to sleep at night. Instead, here in Kibera, this girl is selling things.

ELIZABETH, 18

I am looking forward to achieving my dreams and changing Kibera to make it a better place for every boy and girl. Many people, especially those from poshy areas, look down on residents of Kibera. I am looking forward to changing their negative mentality.

LEONIDAH, 16

« Opposite page: Photo by Elizabeth, 18
« This page: Photo by Faith, 21

What is the best part of being a young woman in Kenya?

To me, the best part of being a young woman in Kenya is to be a good mother to my children, and to be a good leader in my community.

FAITH, 21

Young women are sometimes loved so much in the community, because they care for their families very well.

HALIMA, 17

The best part of being a young woman in Kenya is that you are somebody. We are the ones who give birth, I mean life, to other people. If it wasn't for women, then we would not be living today.

FATUMA, 19

What is the worst part?

Being a teenage mother. It's all stress taking care of a baby when you are also being taken care of by your parents. The society, and even your friends, neglect you. The father of the child dumps you and doesn't provide for his child.

LEONIDAH, 16

The worst part of being a young woman in Kenya is that people think you are property to be used, and not somebody who can do something, like a man.

FATUMA, 19

Being raped is the worst thing to me in Kenya. And not being given respect the way we deserve.

FAITH, 21

The worst part of being a young woman in Kenya is that gender equality is not practiced.

MERCY L., 15

The way we are treated by the men. We are there to be seen, but not to be heard.

ZEBAH, 17

« Opposite page: Photo by Amida, 18

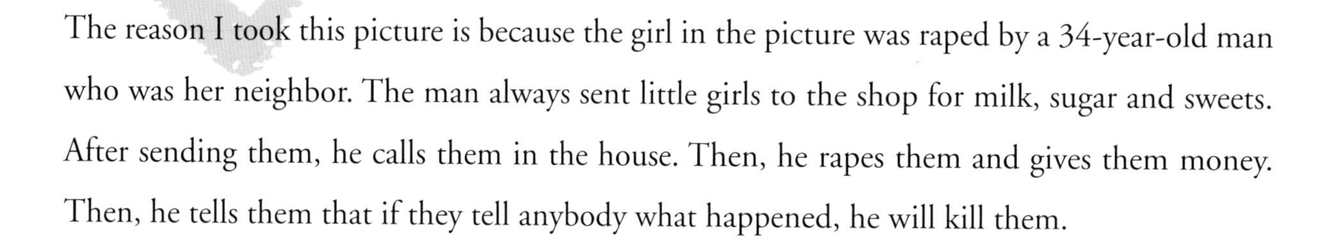

The reason I took this picture is because the girl in the picture was raped by a 34-year-old man who was her neighbor. The man always sent little girls to the shop for milk, sugar and sweets. After sending them, he calls them in the house. Then, he rapes them and gives them money. Then, he tells them that if they tell anybody what happened, he will kill them.

This girl was raped on a Sunday morning, while her mom and dad were away from home at work. Then, on Monday morning, her mom asked her what happened and she explained. The man is jailed for 15 years.

MERCILINE, 17

The man is jailed for 15 years.

Opposite page: Photo by Merciline, 17 »
Following page, left: Photo by Amida, 18 »
Following page, right: Photo by Rosemary, 18 »

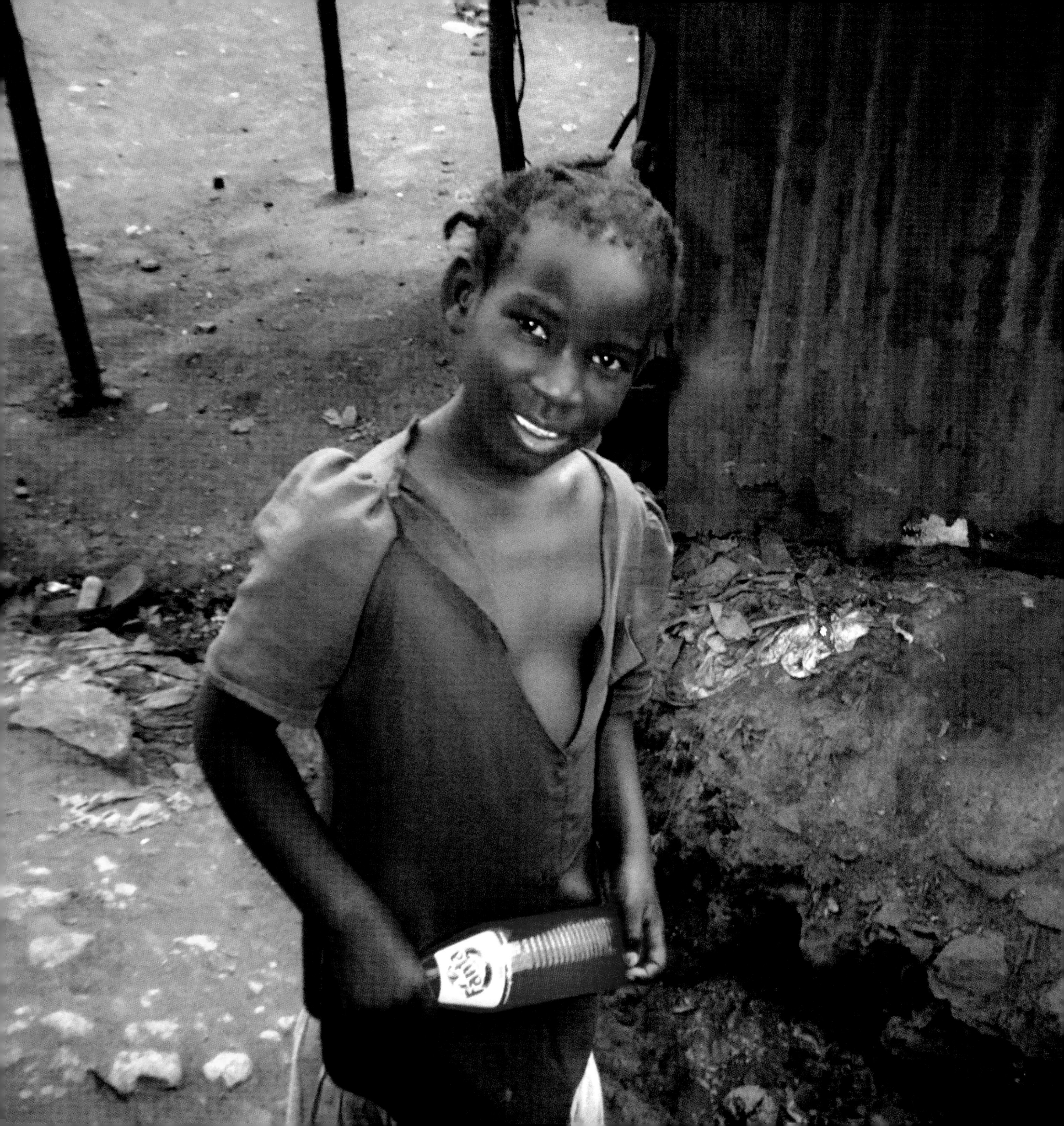

AMIDA, 18

I am a girl. My name is Amida, and don't worry about the nickname. I was born in Kenya and I am a Nubian. I have been raised by my mother since I was born.

My eyes are large and lovely. My hair is smooth and shaggy. My teeth are white and have natural gaps. I am black in color and tall in height. My round face is protruding cheekbones. My hair is busily uncombed and I come from a family of six children and I am the second to last. I live near the mosque, and I am a Muslim.

I am a student. I would like to be an accountant or a lawyer when I grow big. After returning from work, I would like to form a women's club.

« Opposite page: Photo by Amida, 18

How do you feel when parents keep their daughters home from school, but send their sons?

I feel sad because I know that boys and girls are equal and they are both your children. You raised them together so you shouldn't separate them at school.

CELESTINE, 19

I feel hurt because I try to place myself in the shoes of those girls. they are too tight for me, and some are too big for me. That shows how those parents are gender insensitive.

LEONIDAH, 16

I feel like wringing their necks because these children are equal and, in fact, the girl child could even do better than the boy child in school.

HALIMA, 17

I feel really offended and I wish that those parent would be taken to jail.

SIAMA, 15

I feel as if they are betraying the girl, denying her the right to her life and many other things which she could achieve. What I believe is that the man is the head of the house and the woman is the neck. Without her, nothing could support the man. And why not educate her in order for her to help the man when they get married?

FATUMA, 19

It makes me feel lonely as if I could open the underground and place myself there. Because nowadays women are ministers, journalists and other things.

SAUMU, 16

« Opposite page: Photo by Judy M., 18

this picture is about this girl. She is very sad because she does not go to school. She wants to go to school, but her parents said that girls are not supposed to go to school, but they are supposed to stay at home and look after the children and wash clothes and dishes. The girl here wants to learn and be like other girls. She said that she wants to learn so that she can be respected. That is very sad. She said that learning will help her in the future. She said that she can't blame her parents, because her parents are poor. They can't even afford the money for her school fees, even though she wants very much to learn.

She wants her children to go to school someday and understand how it is good to be educated, because education is the key to the future. Education can make you a good lawyer so you can fight for women. She said that if she can go to school and get a good job, she would help the people who are poor.

EMILY, 17

« Opposite page: Photo by Emily,17
» Following pages: Photo by Alice, 17

This picture is a place where some people work and live. It is right near the railway line and this place is very bad because it looks like a horrible dustbin. I can't believe people are working there. We want our place to be clean and look very nice.

CELESTINE, 19

This page: Photo by Celestine, 19 ≈
Opposite page: Photo by Elizabeth, 18 »

Uchumi

MERCY K., 18

My name is Mercy. I'm a girl, age 18 years old. I go to a secondary school which is not far from home. I live in the Kibera community where there are many people who I enjoy seeing. I'm the second girl in our family of six children. I see myself as a very special person.

I want to continue with my school so that I can be so special and famous. My role models are Mother Teresa, Nelson Mandela and all doctors. I want to be like them because I feel it is good to be famous and help those people who are needy.

My favorite food is chapati, rice, matoke and any meat because I feel happy when I eat meat stew. I really like myself because I'm wonderfully made.

« Opposite page: Photo by Mercy K., 18

How does domestic violence make you feel? What do you think should be done to stop it?

I feel it is not good to beat your wife and that it should be stopped and all husbands who beat their wives should be taken to jail so that people understand that violence is not good.

CELESTINE, 19

It makes me feel sick and bad. I would like to teach these people a lesson by taking them to jail or throwing them to the crocodiles.

FAITH, 21

Domestic violence makes me feel like I am not important in the community and I am not liked.

JACQUELINE, 17

Very bad and awful. They should really punish those hooligans. How can they do that to the poor ladies?

HALIMA, 17

It makes me feel sick. I think that people who do it should be stopped and jailed, so that when they come out of prison, they never do it again.

MERCY L., 15

Domestic violence makes me feel like hating all the men in the world. Why punish a woman when she does wrong and why not also punish a man when he does wrong?

FATUMA, 19

It makes me feel bad. To stop it, I think we should educate women on their rights.

ZENAH, 15

It makes me feel very bad, and it should be stopped by teaching everyone about their rights and freedoms.

IRENE, 17

Opposite page: Photo by Mourine A., 18 »

You see, this is my cousin. She is washing the clothes. She is the only girl in the house and she has a big brother. Every day when he comes home from school, he changes out of his school uniform and puts it in the basin. Then he goes and plays football. It is her job to wash his clothes for him, and then also wash the utensils at home. You know, it is not good for girls to do all the work at home. Even boys can fetch water, wash the utensils and do the laundry. Here in Kibera, boys say that girls are the only ones who are supposed to wash the clothes, carry the babies and fetch the water. If you tell a boy to carry a baby, he says, "That is work for girls only!"

ROSEMARY, 18

« Opposite page: Photo by Rosemary, 18
≈ Following pages: Photo by Linnet, 17

MAUREEN W., 17

My name is Maureen, and I am 18 years old. I am a Kikuyu. Our family is made up of 3 – my mother, my sister and me. I am the first born.

My hobbies are reading novels and swimming, but I also like making new friends. I am medium in size and brown in color. I love laughing a lot. I also love my books because I know that education is the key to success. I am planning to be an air hostess in the near future.

My favorite food is rice and chicken. I also like soft drinks. My favorite musicians are Sean Paul, Westlife, and Boys 2 Men. By the way, I love music and dancing a lot.

« Opposite page: Photo by Emily, 17

Men find it difficult to wash their clothes. The woman in this picture's husband makes her do all of the household chores.

In society, men should help their spouses.

Many men find it very hard to do household chores and so they overwork the women. Sometimes, when a woman gets sick, the man should be able to help her with any necessary work.

But some men help their wives. A few of them even cook for their wives. Some men do love their wives very much and they even do housework together.

JUDY M., 18

« Opposite page: Photo by Judy M., 18
≍ Following left page: Photo by Rosemary, 18
≍ Following right page: Photo by Judy W., 17

This page: Photo by Miriam, 19 ≈

Who is your role model?

I respect my mother and I love her so much and she knows all that her children want in life. She works so that her children don't have the problems that others face in life. She works so hard so we have shelter, clothing and we can go to school.

CELESTINE, 19

My mother has always been there for my family, especially my siblings and I. She makes sure that she has brought us up the best way she can. She is the kind of person you can run to in times of problems. She counsels, advises and guides.

LEONIDAH, 16

Although she died last week, I can describe my mother as a main role model through my life when she was alive. She really built me up the most perfect way. She'll forever be the queen of my heart, I love my mom so much. May the almighty rest her soul in eternal peace.

HALIMA, 17

My mother is such a kind and a loving mother that deserves respect. I really appreciate and respect whatever she tells me. That woman is such a wonderful gift.

MERCY K., 18

My mother. She is my role model but I want my future to be brighter than hers. she always works very hard to see her children get the basic needs.

SIAMA, 15

This page: Photo by Gertrude, 16 ≈
Opposite page: Photo by Mourine A., 18 »

WAVES OF GLORY

SUSAN, 17

I'm writing this essay about my life history. When I was born in 1989, I was a beautiful girl and my mom took care of me. When I was eight, my mom told me that my father died when I was young. When my mom told me that, I felt a lot of stress and I didn't want to talk with anybody in school.

So, now I want to learn. I want to work hard in school. When I finish my education, I want to help my mom and my younger brother and sister. I want to get a job and be a lawyer. In my life, I want to continue with Binti Pamoja and help my friends learn about AIDS. Many of the things that I learn about in Binti Pamoja, I teach my fellow friends in school.

« Opposite page: Photo by Elizabeth, 18

≈ This page, left: Photo by Halima, 17
≈ This page, middle, right: Photos by Rosemary, 18

This page, left: Photo by Alice, 17 ≈
This page, middle: Photo by Fatuma, 19 ≈
This page, right: Photo by Stephanie, 17 ≈

I took this picture because this boy does not have a father. His father died when he was a little baby. So, his mother is going from house to house to look for a job to take him to school and feed him. When that boy sees his mother, he is so happy because that is the only parent that the boy has. This boy knows that his mother is very sad and even the boy has started to be sad. So everyday, the woman wakes up very early in the morning to go and find anything for her child to eat, because her son is the only hope. She would rather sleep without eating if her son could eat. As the wise men said, there is no person in the world like a mother.

EMILY, 17

« Opposite page: Photo by Miriam, 19
⌃ This page: Photo by Emily, 17

What do you think is the solution to poverty in Kenya?

Working together as a nation and planning for the future. We must elect responsible leaders.

LEONIDAH, 16

The formation of jobs. This will make people employed and make people have money.

JACQUELINE, 17

Enhance our living standards. We beg the Kenyan government to help the slum dwellers please.

HALIMA, 17

The solution to poverty in Kenya is family planning. With family planning, people will have children that they can take care of. The government then should be able to provide jobs for the small population. Another thing is to provide the best method of farming so that we have enough food so it will stop us from depending on developed countries.

FATUMA, 19

The poor people should be given money by the government to start businesses. The youths should go to school so that they better their lives.

SIAMA, 15

« Opposite page: Photo by Judy M., 18

MAMA
KIMBO
KASUKU

The woman in the picture works with Nairobi City Council, but they don't pay her salary on time to feed her five children. So, she has to also sell charcoal and paraffin in order to get enough to buy food for her children. Before the husband died, there were no problems and there was enough money for the family to feed on. But after the death of the husband, she faced a lot of problems. She decided to sell the charcoal in order to get enough money to pay school fees and rent. In such a family, life is very difficult. Especially when there were two people helping one another, but one died. Such families sometimes end up with many problems, like children not going to school.

FATUMA, 19

« Opposite page: Photo by Fatuma, 19

UNTIL

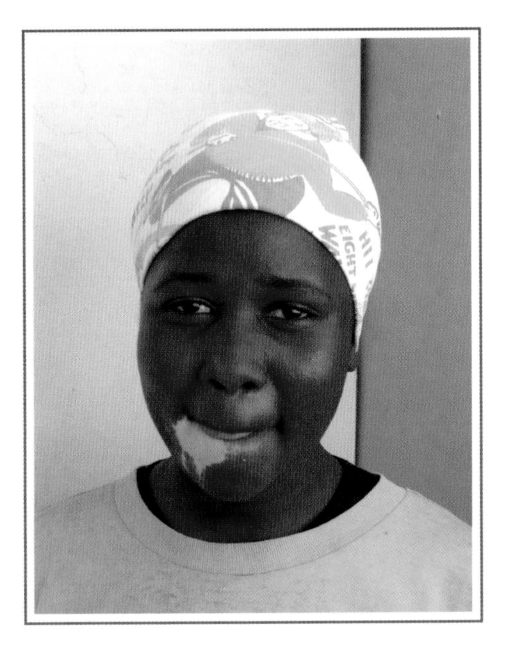

KADARA, 16

My name is Kadara. I'm 16 years old. My favorite subjects are math and English. I like reading magazines. I live with my mother. My father died. I have one sister and three brothers. When school is closed, I help my mother by doing the house work. Sometimes I go to visit my friends.

When I finish primary school, I want to continue with my studies until I finish school. When I grow up, I want to be a pilot. I want to take care of my mother the way she has cared for me since my father died. My mother is struggling to feed us. She is doing a small business in order to get money. My sister finished primary school, but due to lack of fees, she did not continue with school like my brother.

« Opposite page: Photo by Kadara, 16

If you could change anything about your life in Kibera, what would it be?

I want to be a leader in my community and change girl's lives and make them understand that they are very important people in this world and they can make it.

CELESTINE, 19

I would change the lifestyle of young women in Kibera. Many young women living in Kibera suffer a lot from early marriage and domestic violence.

MERCY L., 15

If I could change my life in Kibera, I would change the way we live and the structure of the houses for our environment and our health. I would like to change these because if our houses were changed then Kibera would no longer be a slum and everything would change. Even people's attitude toward Kibera would change.

FATUMA, 19

I would change my living standard because, here in Kibera, our living standard is so poor and I hope to change it and have a better life in my future. I think that is my dream.

ZENAH, 15

I would make sure that all the children are in school and live in better conditions as health is concerned. This is because without good health, there is breakage of diseases and more people are dying, and maybe they are the ones who could change this place. Also, I would make sure that no woman or girl is mistreated through rape or wife beating and no child is submitted to forced labor.

PHYLIS, 18

My living standard and my education because it is horrible. I do not like the life which I am living in and the education is very scarce.

ALICE, 17

« Opposite page: Photo by Zebah, 17

Life in Kibera as a young woman is terrible and full of problems. The days for me do not have any difference. They are just the same. Worries and problems. I feel a lot of stress and feel unwanted and poor. There is nothing I like about living in Kibera because life here is difficult. Poorness. Hazard. Drugs. HIV victims. Thugs. It's terrible living here in Kibera.

FAITH, 21

« Opposite page: Photo by Faith, 21
≈ This page: Photo by Elizabeth, 18

water is a problem in parts of the slums. Us girls, we are not being given our rights. In this picture, you see a girl carrying water. This girl is a maid. Everyday in the morning she is sent to this neighborhood outside of Kibera to bring water when it is very cold. After she has been given the money, she goes to her friends and asks them for a place to sleep. Her stepmother is cruel to her and she is always afraid because she was beaten and thrown out in the cold.

MERCILINE, 17

Opposite page: Photo by Merciline, 17 »

Rina

HALIMA, 17

My name is Halima, and I stay with my parents. I usually go to school very early in the morning when the frost has not yet departed. I am black, but not as black as charcoal, and I am tall, but not as tall as a giraffe.

I live in the Kibera slums. I have four brothers and two sisters, plus my dad and mom. That makes nine members in our family. My hobby is collecting stamps. My name does not have a meaning.

My favorite sports are boxing, karate and gymnastics. I also like ballet and am practicing to be a ballerina (just for fun). My favorite musicians are Eminem, Eve, Burning Spear, Culture and Missy Elliott. I also kind of like rock and roll and Marilyn Manson (but I don't like his looks). My main ambition when I grow up is to join the armed forces.

« Opposite page: Photo by Halima, 17

This picture shows a young girl in Kibera playing in a very dirty place. The running water there is very dirty. What should we do as youth in Kibera? Should we just watch our younger sisters and brothers playing in the dirty water? They will be sick because they touch the dirty water and sometimes even drink it.

MERCILINE, 17

This page: Photo by Merciline, 17 ≈
Opposite page: Photo by Judy W., 17 »

Previous pages: Photo by Merciline, 17 ≈
This page: Photo by Gertrude, 16 ≈
Opposite page: Photo by Amida, 18 »

This picture shows some pupils playing football in a dusty field. They like playing football. It is one of their best hobbies. The only problem that we have is that we have no proper field. Secondly, the one that is available is dusty or muddy during the dry and rainy seasons. We often suffer from coughs and colds because of our environment. These boys are hardworking in class. They don't play this game during lessons, but they do it during game time and during brief breaks that they are given.

AMIDA, 18

FATUMA, 19

I am Fatuma, a student at Langata High School. After I finish my high school, I know, since I have faith in my studies, that I will be able to go to a university, which will help me see my future plans fulfilled. In my family, we have five children, two boys and three girls. I am 19 years old and the third born in my family. My family has a single parent since my dad died in the year 1998. Thank God my mother was there for us. She is the father and also the mother in my family. She works hard to see that her children are in school, eating well, and dressing nicely. My mother is my best friend. Without her, I would not be the real Fatuma that you see or laugh with.

In Kibera, life is very challenging, especially if you are a girl. I am afraid of going out during the night because somebody could come and do something to ruin the rest of your life.

« Opposite page: Photo by Fatuma, 19

What is the best way to stop AIDS in Kibera?

It's all about oneself. Everyone should understand that it's their duty to take care of their lives. The youth in Kibera should be taught about self-awareness. This will urge them to be assertive, especially girls. Young women must have their own principles and be assertive. When they say no, let them mean it. And life shall go on.

LEONIDAH, 16

Young women should educate the world about AIDS, the problems it has caused and how much it kills.

AZRA, 16

The best way to stop AIDS in Kibera is by teaching and doing more campaigning. This way, people will have more information on the disease and know how to prevent it. That is the easiest way to stop AIDS in Kibera.

FATUMA, 19

I would tell men that what is happening is real and AIDS can be stopped by women and men together. Together, we can make it.

FAITH, 21

« Opposite page: Photo by Judy W., 17

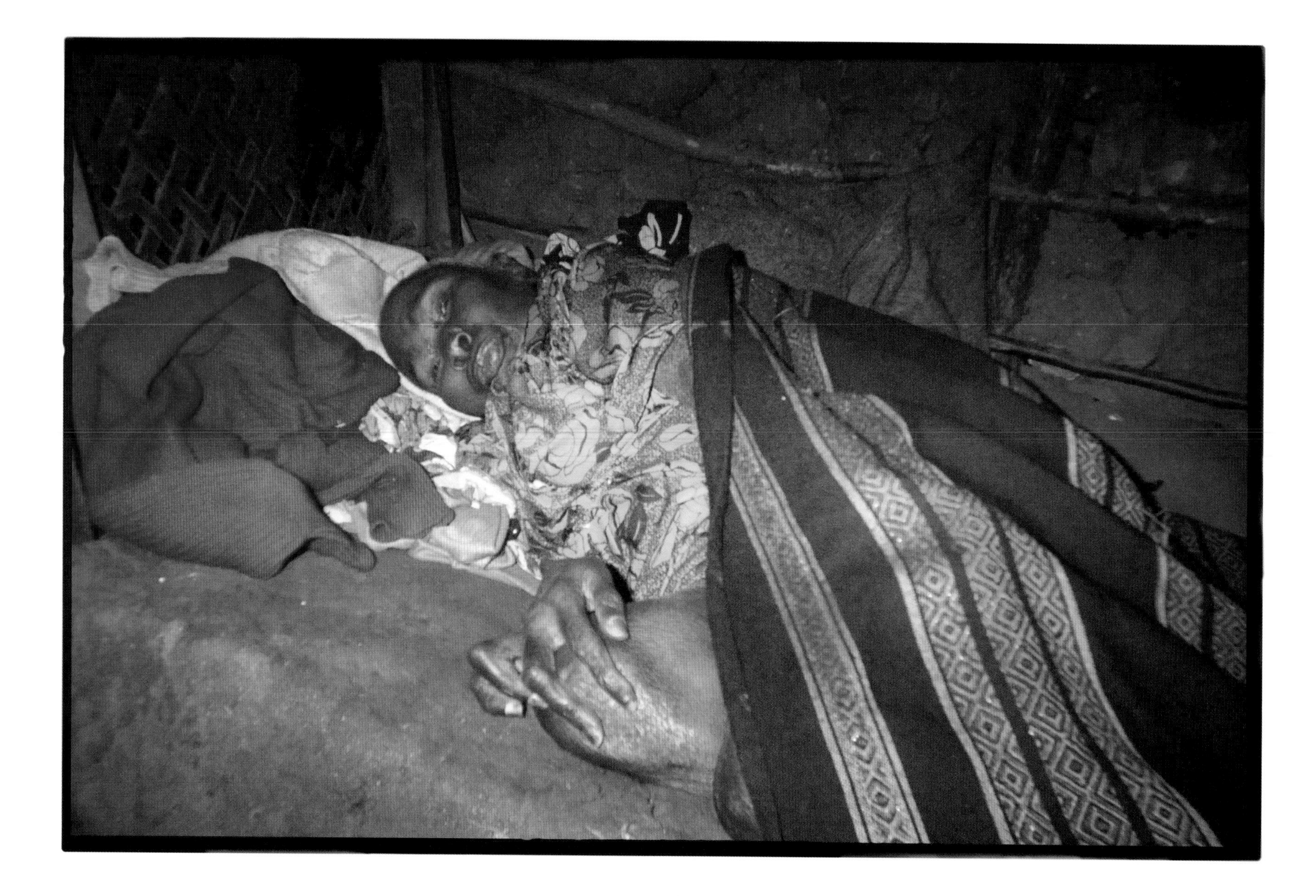

This picture is Muturi's grandmother. This old mother has had the AIDS virus for ten years. The reason I took this picture was because the grandmother lives with her two grandchildren. One is called Njoki and another is Muturi. Her husband died a long time ago because of the AIDS virus. Also, these children's parents died a long time ago. Even Njoki now has a child who is one year old, but they are still living with their grandmother. Muturi is working. He provides food for the family. Njoki does not work. She provides food for the family by doing prostitution. As her neighbors, we advise her against this because it can cause HIV.

ZEBAH, 17

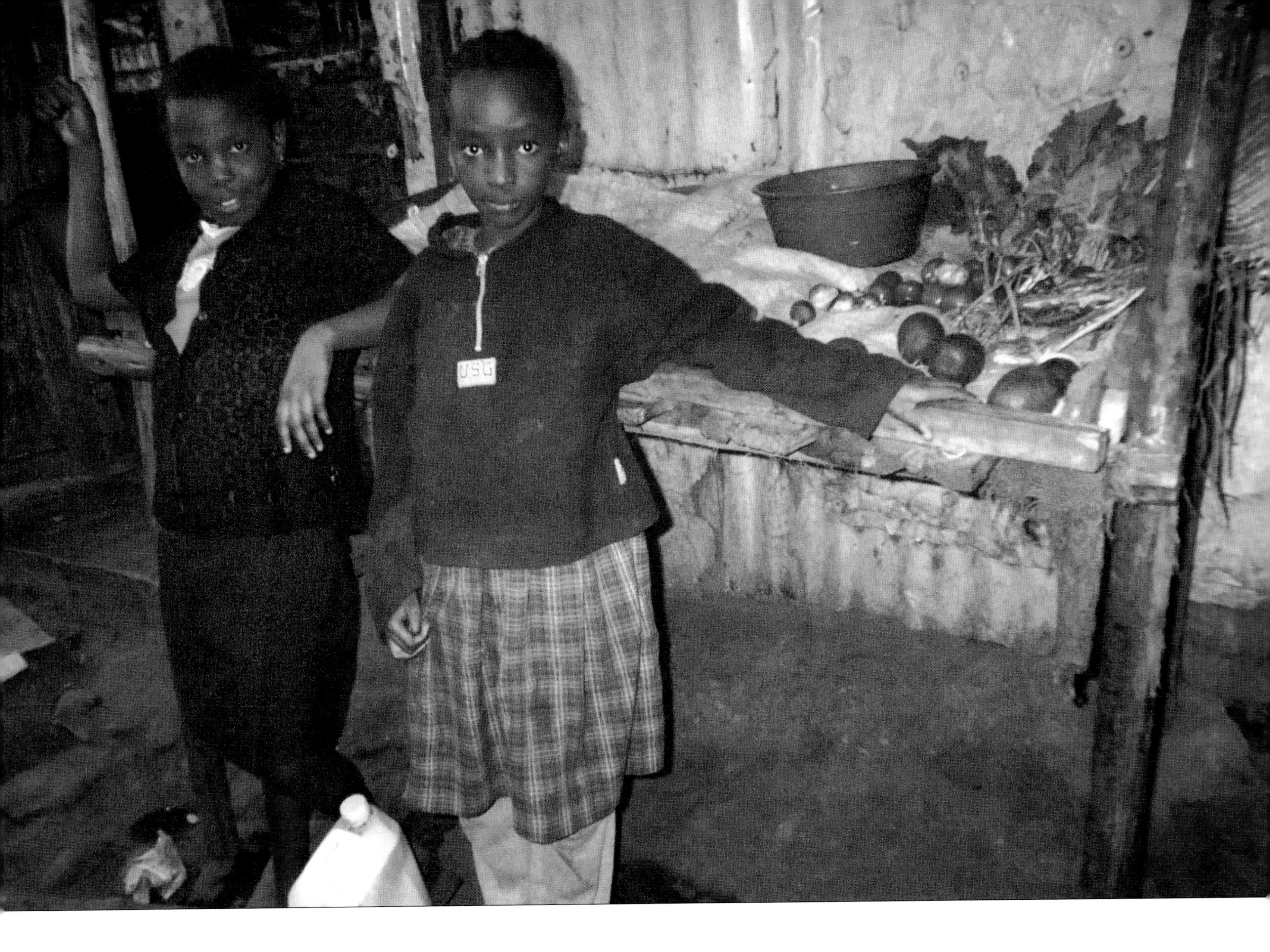

Being a young woman in Kibera means a lot. First, poverty is the common thing in Kibera. It leads to prostitution. As a young woman in Kibera, I don't prefer this life. So, the most important thing is to be responsible and a hard working young woman. First, you make yourself smart. Then you make yourself healthy.

ZEBAH, 17

≈These pages: Photos by Zebah, 17

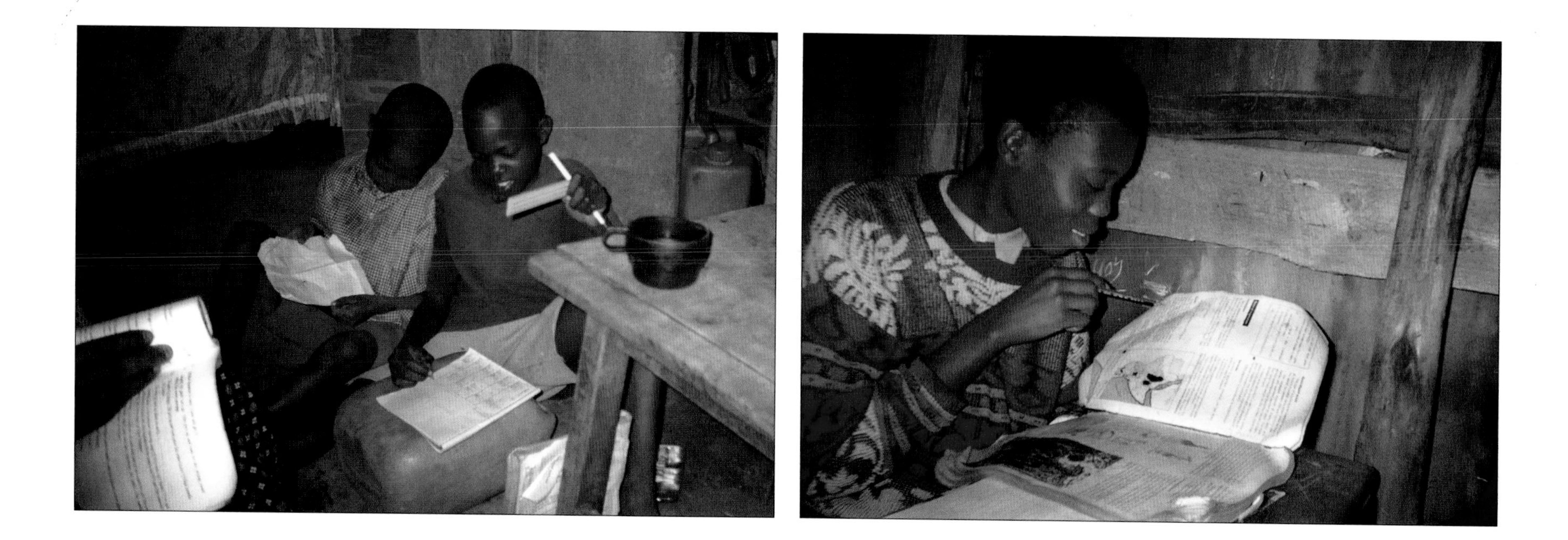

My hope for the future is that, when I grow up, I would like to become a doctor so that I can treat other people when they feel sick, and also offer free medication for the ones who dont have the money.

HALIMA, 17

≈ This page, left: Photo by Gertrude, 16
≈ This page, right: Photo by Rosemary, 18

In Kibera, most people say that girls are not supposed to go to school. But that is not fair, because even women are supposed to go to school. We are career women and we have our own rights. We have a right to go to school. If I had a chance, I would tell people to let girls go to school because I don't see how we can survive without learning. If we depend on men, I don't see how we can survive. So, that is a problem with life in Kibera. I would like to have an office someday. Parents should know that it is a wild violence not to take girls to school. If you see that your friends are going to school and you are not going, you feel ashamed.

ALICE, 17

This page: Photos by Rosemary, 18 ≈

If you walk along the road, you will see that only women are selling vegetables. Men are doing the good work that can give them money. Millions and billions, and then they are called the breadwinners. We are the same in every way. We can work like them, we can walk like them – except that they are stronger.

Why is it that women are not given a chance to make our dreams come true? Instead of us doing what we want, we are forced to do what we don't want to do. If we refuse, we are beaten to death.

Some men are very bad. After making you pregnant, he will tell you that he is going to work and then he will not come back. So, you go on with your small business, and when he comes home, he beats you and leaves you there without help. Maybe, if it is at night, you will be afraid to call on your neighbors and you will wait until the next day.

In this picture here, you see a woman doing a small business, and she is pregnant. After her husband knew that she was pregnant, she was beaten. Her husband denied that the child was his and left her there with nobody to lean on. After that, she went to the hospital. When she was tested, they found that she had AIDS.

Now she is struggling for her life. The only thing that she can depend on is her small business. Everyone is afraid to buy her cut vegetables, because they think that maybe she cut herself and the blood went in the vegetables.

MERCILINE, 17

≈ This page: Photo by Merciline, 17
» Opposite page: Photo by Emily, 17

this boy is very sad because he has no place to go. His parents beat him every day and so he ran out of the house, which is very bad. It is bad for parents to beat their children.

EMILY, 17

EMILY, 17

My name is Emily. I come from Makina, a village in Kibera. I am tall and slim and not very brown in color. Emily means "Every Minute I Love You."

I like being a girl because I want to know my rights. I want to teach other girls their rights also, so that they can be respected. If I grow up, I would like to be a lawyer and to help people.

« Opposite page: Photo by Rosemary, 18

What do you want to be when you grow up?

A surgeon, pharmacist or doctor. Since my childhood, I have loved anything to do with biomedicine. And I feel good serving other people. And, until now, that fire is still burning inside me.

LEONIDAH, 16

I want to be a musician, actor, business woman, and at the same time work with an NGO. I want to help those who can not make it on their own or achieve their goals.

FAITH, 21

I would like to be a journalist and a musician. This is because I am talented in singing.

JACQUELINE, 17

I want to join the armed forces, because they defend the country.

HALIMA, 17

I would like to be like Mother Teresa, because she helped the poor and orphans and gave them food and clothes.

MERCY L., 15

A president so that I can uplift the lives of our people living in the slum.

SIAMA, 15

I want to be more than one thing in my life when I grow up. I want to be a lawyer in order to help women. I want to be an accountant in order to work in a bank. And I want to be a politician in order to challenge men in parliament. And lastly, I want to be an author and write as many books as I can about my future and fellow women.

FATUMA, 19

An accountant. I will deal with money most of the time, and I will make sure that any money given out goes to the right and legal project. I will be in the front line of helping to fight corruption.

PHYLIS, 18

I would like to be a nurse so that I may help my young sister and brother and also my mother.

PAULINE, 15

« Opposite page: Photo by Merciline, 17

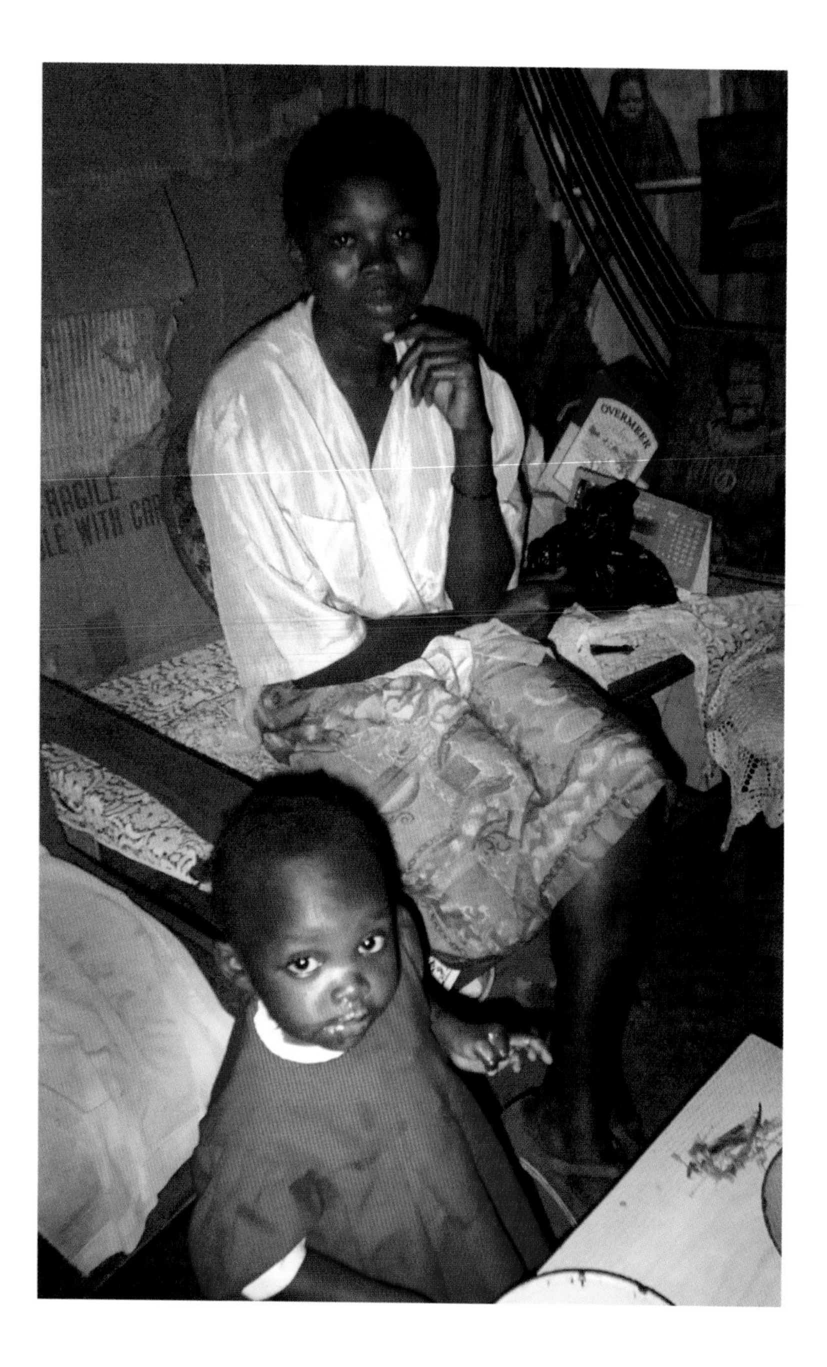

I know a girl who is a prostitute. She finishes her homework first, so that when 9:00 p.m. comes, she can go sell her little body so that she can pay her school fees. Sometimes she dances naked and sometimes she does prostitution. Then, she goes to find food in the dustbins when she does not even have a cent.

HALIMA, 17

This is our house. The mother is breastfeeding the baby because he is hungry. The other things are house utensils. It is one o'clock so the girl is trying to cook some porridge so they can drink.

MIRIAM, 19

« Opposite page: Photo by Faith, 21
⌃ This page: Photo by Miriam, 19

This picture demonstrates a heap of rubbish deposited by the river. This is done by people who say they are law abiding citizens. However, what they say is not what they actually do. It is clear that this kind of contamination can cause horrible diseases, including dysentery, malaria, cholera, and typhoid. Some of these diseases are beyond human knowledge. So, it's better for the people who are doing this to stop. As we can see, the picture shows that the place is very dirty and a breeding place for mosquitoes. The children who live there are always sick with diseases. Some people in Kibera don't boil water for drinking. As you can see, most of the water pipes pass through that dirty place. Sometimes, you find that the water pipe has a hole and all of the dirtiness enters through the hole and into the water pipes.

AMIDA, 18

≈ This page, left, right: Photos by Amida, 18
≈ This page, center: Photo by Mary, 15
« Opposite page: Photo by Mary, 15

keppel

As a young girl who lives in Kibera and faces many problems, I think Kibera is developing. Our Member of Parliament, Raila Odinga, remembered us. He built a bridge, which is shown in the picture above.

Before that bridge, it was a big problem for us to cross from one side to the other, because of the big trench. It is sad to say this, but during the rainy season, we lost approximately 10 people in that area because the water would drown people when they were trying to cross. I think our cry has finally been heard, because the bridge has finally been built and there are no more problems of crossing to the other side.

FATUMA, 19

« Opposite page, top: Photo by Gertrude, 16
« Opposite page, bottom: Photo by Zebah, 17
≈ This page: Photo by Fatuma, 19

This little girl is coming from her house. She has to pass dirty places. This place is where people throw garbage. This place is not pleasing even to look at. This is where they live. If it is the rainy season, the houses are swept away. The landlord rebuilds them again because they are made of mud, so they are cheap to build.

Last year, there was a boy who was swept away by the rain in this place after he tried to cross to the other end. He was found dead in the middle of the houses. A very old woman discovered his body, which was floating in the water.

When I saw this little girl, I felt sorry because she was crossing and jumping over the garbage. This place is where people dump their children after having an abortion. One time when I was going to school, I noticed a box that was floating in the water. I took a stick and opened it. To my surprise, it was a baby who had not yet developed.

MERCY K., 18

Opposite page: Photo by Mercy K., 18 »

STD
Mende + mende =

Is it important for you to go to school?

If I didn't go to school, my life would be ruined. I would have to be married and have kids, and I would suffer from being beaten because I don't have any knowledge from school.

CELESTINE, 19

If I did not go to school, all my dreams would be shattered and I would be doing nothing in the world, because without education, there's nowhere I can go.

KADARA, 16

Yes, it is very important because I can get knowledge and can understand how life goes. I enjoy being in school with my friends and my teachers. I help my friends who have problems with reproductive health and HIV/AIDS.

CELESTINE, 19

Yes, it is important to me to go to school because educating a woman is to educate a nation.

FAITH, 21

Yes. We all know education is the key to success, and when I go to school I am very sure that I'll get what I want in the future.

SIAMA, 15

It is most important to go to school. Without it, one would not succeed in life. I say that because almost all of my career depends on my education. What I believe is that with education, I can do what others have not done and change the world.

FATUMA, 19

Yes, by going to school, I gain knowledge that is important for the rest of my life. With the help of education, I'll be able to change the life I live in Kibera.

AZRA, 16

« Opposite page: Photo by Zebah, 17

Women

Women in Kibera find it hard to bring up their children due to the lack of support from their husbands. Hence, they end up carrying firewood for sale. This is a very hard job because they end up being caught by forest rangers. The rangers sometimes ask for bribes, and if the women don't have money, the women pay with their bodies. They are raped. Due to the forest rangers taking these bribes, this leads to the decline of the national economy. It also encourages deforestation, STD's and HIV/AIDS.

These women develop problems in their bodies, such as backaches. But, without doing this work, they would have no income to help themselves.

Some problems arise when they have not sold their firewood. They end up starving, and their children are chased from school. This brings frustration and stress to these women. The small money they get is not enough for their daily needs.

JUDY M., 18

« Opposite page: Photo by Judy M., 18

How have you changed since you became a member of Binti Pamoja?

I have changed drastically from a young girl to a responsible woman. I learned that you can get pregnant the first time you have sex.

HALIMA, 17

What I have learned since I started Binti Pamoja is not to be shy.

MERCY L., 15

I have gained confidence and my self-esteem has grown to the highest level, where it is supposed to be.

ZEBAH, 17

I used to think negatively about myself. But, through Binti Pamoja, I am now changed and I am no longer as shy as I used to be.

PHYLIS, 18

I have learned that, if you are raped, you should tell your parents. If you have not told them, you may have a problem.

SHARON, 13

I have learned so much. I even feel like my head is going to blow. Binti Pamoja is really sweet.

ZABIBA, 13

I have really changed my attitude toward HIV and AIDS. In the past, I really was afraid of socializing with people who were suffering. But now, I am bold enough and have courage to face them.

MERCY K., 18

Opposite page: Photo by Merciline, 17 »

My Life in Kibera as a young woman: I should be given my rights, and as I talk, I should be listened to. That way, when there is something wrong or if somebody does anything that hurts me, I can say it without fear.

JUDY W., 17

This page: Photo by Rosemary, 18 ≈
Opposite page: Photo by Gertrude, 16 »

This is how women in Kibera get their daily bread. In Kibera, women are so hard-working and self-dependent. Some women in Kibera have husbands, but when the husbands get their salaries, they are nowhere to be seen, so it forces the mother to need other means of getting money. That is why women are seen everywhere in Kibera doing small businesses. They even sometimes find it difficult to cope with their husbands because, when the man sees a woman with money, they are always beaten because the husband thinks that they have been with other men. So, sometimes their business doesn't help them.

JUDY M., 18

« Opposite page: Photo by Judy M., 18
≍ Following page: Photo by Emily, 17
≍ Following page: Essay by Fatuma, 19

I am a young upcoming woman
and a leader of tomorrow.
of tomorrow